Beginner's Guide to
Mountmellick
Embroidery

This book is dedicated to my mother, who passed her love of
stitchery on to me, and to my husband and family who have
given me freedom and allowed me to 'do my own thing'.
Nothing I have ever achieved would have been possible
without their support and encouragement.

Beginner's Guide to
Mountmellick
Embroidery

Pat Trott

SEARCH PRESS

First published in Great Britain 2002

Search Press Limited
Wellwood, North Farm Road,
Tunbridge Wells, Kent TN2 3DR

Reprinted 2004, 2006, 2009, 2011,2012

Text copyright © Pat Trott 2002
Embroidery designs copyright © Pat Trott 2002

Photographs by Charlotte de la Bédoyère, Search Press Studios
Photographs and design copyright © Search Press Ltd. 2002

ISBN: 978 085532 919 8

The Publishers and author can accept no responsibility for any
consequences arising from the information, advice or instructions
given in this publication.

Readers are permitted to reproduce any of the embroideries in
this book for their personal use, or for the purposes of selling for
charity, free of charge and without the prior permission of the
Publishers. Any use of the embroideries for commercial purposes is
not permitted without the prior permission of the Publishers.

Suppliers
If you have difficulty in obtaining any of the materials and
equipment mentioned in this book, then please write to the
Publishers, at the address above, for a current list of stockists,
including firms who operate a mail-order service.

*I would like to thank Pam Watts for introducing and
recommending me to Roz Dace, and Roz for having
faith in me and persuading me to try something I
thought I could never accomplish.*

*My grateful thanks to my son-in-law, Richard, who
is always ready to make frames of any size I ask for.*

*I would also like to thank all at Search Press,
especially Sophie, for their help and kindness, and Lotti
for the beautiful photographs.*

*Finally a very big thank you to all my friends
and students for their invaluable support and
encouragement; when things got tough they were the
ones that kept me going.*

Publisher's note
All the step-by-step photographs in this book feature the
author, Pat Trott, demonstrating Mountmellick embroidery.
No models have been used.

Printed in Malaysia by Times Offset (M) Sdn Bhd

Contents

Introduction

Mountmellick embroidery employs many stitches and, as I consider myself to be a traditional hand stitcher, I think that is the reason I love it so much. I am never happier than when I have a needle in my hand and am creating an article that contains numerous stitches. If I have had a bad day at the office, the way I de-stress is to sit in a comfy chair, pick up a needle and start to stitch by hand.

My mother gave me my love of embroidery. She was Armenian and was brought up to be industrious, never idle, and to make items for her dowry, for the day she got married and set up home with her new husband. She passed her love of embroidery down to me, and now I hope to share my passion for stitches with you.

Although I already knew a lot of the stitches used, I discovered Mountmellick embroidery when studying for a course. Now that I teach embroidery, I realise that this technique is an ideal way to introduce it to newcomers, as they can concentrate on learning lots of stitches without having to worry about colour. Mountmellick is always white on white, and its beauty is shown to advantage by the way the light falls on the sculptured stitchery.

Mountmellick embroidery was introduced to Ireland during the nineteenth century by Johanna Carter (c.1830), a member of the Society of Friends. It was developed in the town of Mountmellick in County Laois. The production of this technique was set up as a cottage industry to help the women of families affected by famine to earn some money. Readily available fabric and threads were used, and useful household items were made. The fabric available was stout cotton twill, which had a sheen, and is now called cotton sateen, or cotton satin jean. The thread used was a matte twisted cotton yarn. Designs were taken from nature, from looking at the surrounding countryside, and were mainly floral.

The Mountmellick technique is very bold and textured, and can be recognised by the following characteristics:

- It is always white on white.
- There are no drawn threads, open work spaces, or eyelets.
- It has contrast: smooth satin stitch against padded and knotted stitchery; and cotton satin fabric against the more matte cotton embroidery thread.
- Fairly large-scale, natural floral designs.
- There is often a buttonholed edge and a knitted fringe, which helps to carry the weight of the heavy embroidery to the edge of the design, and gives a feeling of balance.

I hope I have whetted your appetite, and that you will enjoy the voyage of discovery upon which you are about to embark. Do not be afraid to start: try something small to begin with, so that you will be able to start a larger project with confidence when you feel ready.

Hand embroidery is slow and takes time, even when you know the stitches. It is even slower when you are learning, so do not rush things – just enjoy the learning process.

This book contains a variety of designs, from small individual motifs to larger projects. The small motifs illustrate certain stitches and can be used on their own for a small mat, or combined on a larger item such as a cushion cover or table mat. To gain confidence, you could start by embroidering a small motif, but after all, what is a larger project? Just lots of small motifs joined together. So, gather your materials, get comfortable, pick up your needle and enjoy creating something beautiful.

Good luck and enjoy the journey.

Opposite
This convolvulus design is typical of traditional Mountmellick: it is white on white, and the contrast is provided by the matte cotton thread against the sheen of the fabric. Many different stitches are used to create the bold shapes, inspired by nature.

Materials

Fabric

Mountmellick embroidery requires a closely woven, heavy, **cotton sateen** fabric. It needs to be heavy enough to support the weight of the stitches, especially when working on a large project. This fabric can be obtained from specialist shops, but if you have difficulty, then buy a good quality heavy cotton. Fabrics you can use include **white jean**, **drill**, **twill** and **cotton duck**. You must not be able to see the weave of the fabric, as this will distract you when stitching.

To be on the safe side, you should pre-wash the fabric before you transfer the design on to it. This will remove any residual dressing and shrink the fabric. This is especially important if you are making an item that will require constant washing. When you have spent hours producing a beautiful work of art, it is heartbreaking if it shrinks in the first wash and the whole thing puckers.

Make sure you buy enough fabric to allow for mounting on to a frame while working, and also to leave enough room from the edge of your embroidery to the edge of the finished item. It is best not to embroider right up to the very edge of a piece of work – leave a little fabric between the finished embroidery and the buttonholed hem and knitted fringe.

Threads

Traditionally Mountmellick was worked with a matte cotton thread, but these days we have to use what we can get! It is important to have contrast in your work, so if you have managed to obtain a fabric with a slight sheen, then embroider with matte threads. If your fabric has no sheen, then you can afford to stitch with a mercerised thread that has a little sheen, for instance, perle cotton. Suitable threads can include perle, coton à broder, embroidery soft, craft cotton and some crochet cottons. I do not recommend stranded cotton for this particular technique, but a single, twisted thread.

Perle cotton comes in four thicknesses – 3, 5, 8 and 12. The thickest is 3 and 12 is the finest. This is a mercerised thread.

Coton à broder (in white) comes in six thicknesses – 12, 16, 20, 25, 30 and 35; 12 being the thickest and 35 being the finest. This is also a mercerised thread.

Embroidery soft comes in just one thickness and is a matte cotton.

Craft cotton is usually quite thick, and may be too thick for embroidery. You may use it occasionally if working on a large design, but it is best kept for knitting the fringe of a large project such as a bedspread or tablecloth.

When I say **crochet cotton**, I do not mean the small balls of highly twisted thread that is used to crochet doilies or for tatting – I mean the larger balls of mercerised thread sold in knitting shops. Crochet cotton looks like perle, but you should use a shorter length, as it is not manufactured to stitch with, so will become worn and fluffy when pulled through the fabric too many times. This comes in a variety of thicknesses; a number 5 is quite good.

Purchase a variety of thicknesses of thread so that you have a lovely 'goody bag' to dip into. There is nothing more frustrating than not having the thread you need when you want to start embroidering.

Frames

I work on a frame, as this keeps the fabric taut, and leaves both hands free to work the stitches. You can sit at a table, with the frame propped between your lap and the table, but I like to have a stand on which I can clamp my frame, as this holds it very stable. There are many choices of stand available on the market. I have a solid metal one with a clamp that can accommodate frames from small to large equally well. You can sit almost anywhere to use it, even in the sitting room with the rest of the family, as it just slots in under whatever chair you sit in.

Attaching the fabric to the frame is called 'dressing the frame', and I explain how to dress two different types of frame on pages 39–41.

Clockwise from the right: a seat frame; a large slate frame; a tambour frame with an adjustable screw and home-made square frames, made for me by my son-in-law to the sizes I require.

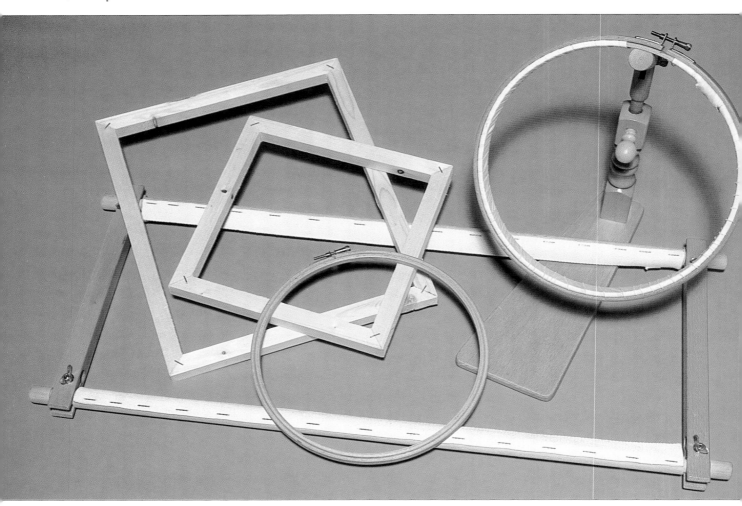

Tambour or round frame

These are available in a variety of sizes, from 7.5cm (3in) to 30.5cm (12in), measured across the middle of the frame. The frame consists of two wooden rings that fit inside one another. The outer ring has an adjustable screw to enable you to tighten it around the inner ring to keep the fabric taut.

Slate frame

A slate frame has two rollers to which webbing is attached, and two side bars with a slot at both ends into which the rollers fit. These frames are made in various sizes, being measured along the length of the webbing. The fabric to be used must not be any wider than the webbing, but the length can be greater than the length of the side bars as the surplus fabric may be wound around the rollers.

I like to work on a frame large enough to show the whole design at once. If this is not possible, at least use a slate frame so that you can see the width of the design and can roll the fabric when the length of it is too long to fit on the frame.

Home-made frame

My son-in-law makes me wooden frames, much like picture frames, to the size I require. They are made from lengths of soft wood, mitred at the corners and then glued and stapled together. If you can make frames like this for yourself, or if you know someone who can do this for you, it is a boon.

Seat frame

It is an advantage to have both hands free when stitching, particularly when executing stitches such as French knots. A seat frame enables you to do this, as it has a flat 'foot' that can be placed under your leg to keep it steady while you are stitching. The seat frame is made up of two parts: a tambour frame fixed to a wooden rod, which is slotted into another hollow piece of wood and held in place with a screw.

Note

Bias binding around the inner ring of a tambour frame holds the fabric more firmly and stops it slipping between the two rings. It also prevents the wood from marking the fabric.

Needles

I will not give specific sizes of needle, as of course it will depend on the thickness of the thread for the project you are working on. Choose a needle with a large enough eye that you can thread easily.

I would use either a chenille needle or a crewel needle. **Chenille needles** come in sizes 18 to 24 and have larger eyes than crewel needles, are slightly thicker and are ideal to stitch with when using a heavy duty cotton fabric, as they go through the fabric more easily when using a thick thread.

Crewel needles are finer, come in sizes 3 to 10 and are ideal when using a fine thread. Both types of needle have a sharp point. Again, gather a collection of sizes so that you have the correct size of needle for the thread you are using.

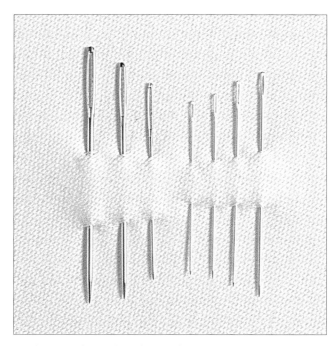

A selection of crewel and chenille needles suitable for Mountmellick embroidery. Choose a size with an eye large enough for the thickness of thread you have chosen.

Other items

Scissors

You need three pairs of scissors: **dressmaking shears** to cut the fabric, **embroidery scissors** to cut the thread, **paper scissors** for cutting greaseproof paper, masking tape and sticky tape.

Bias binding

This will be used to bind the inner ring of a tambour frame, to keep the fabric from slipping and to prevent the wood from marking it.

Crochet cotton

This is used to sew the fabric to the webbing on a slate frame, and to lace the sides of the fabric to the sides of the frame.

Masking tape or sticky tape

This is used to tape the design to a light source, either a light box or a window, and to tape the fabric over the design ready to trace it. I prefer sticky tape as it holds the design and fabric more firmly.

Greaseproof paper

This is used to trace your design on to, either from a book or from a photocopy.

Black pen

This is used to trace the design on to the greaseproof paper. It needs to be a black pen, otherwise you will be unable to see the design through the fabric.

Water soluble marker pen

You will find this pen in most haberdashery shops. It is used to trace the design on to the fabric, and the blue marks it makes can be removed with cold water when the project is complete. Be careful not to buy an air soluble pen, as the marks made disappear in air, often before you have time to finish a project. DO NOT IRON the marks made with water soluble pen, as heat will fix the lines. Also, test it on the edge of your fabric before you trace all the design. Just draw a small line on the edge of the fabric, then try to remove it by touching it with a paint brush dipped in cold water. If it comes out easily, go ahead and trace the whole design.

Paint brush and cold water

When you have finished your embroidery, leave it stretched on the frame, and very carefully touch each design line with a clean paint brush dipped in cold water. Magically, all the blue disappears and you are left with a lovely white embroidery.

Knitting needles

For creating the knitted fringes that go round the edges of many Mountmellick embroideries (see pages 34–37).

Staple gun

This is used to staple the fabric to the frame if you are using the home-made 'picture frame' type of frame described on page 11.

Drawing pins or silk pins

These can be used to attach the fabric to a home-made frame if you do not have a staple gun.

Screwdriver

This is used to loosen the staples and lift them out of the frame when you have finished the embroidery. Usually only one side of the staple comes out.

Pliers

These are used to remove the staples from the frame after loosening them as above.

Tape measure

This is used to measure the fabric before cutting. Allow enough room round the edge of the design to attach the fabric to the frame.

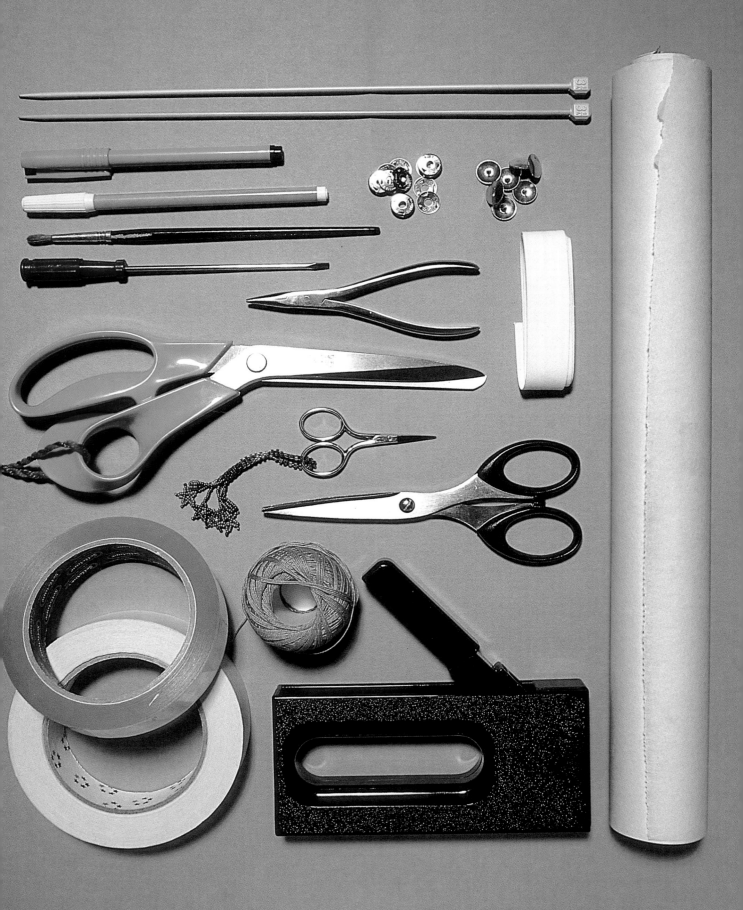

Work station

I like to work on a frame which is being held in a stand. There are many stands available. I have a metal Lowery stand. This consists of a footplate that can slot under any chair you are sitting in to keep the stand stable, an adjustable pole so that your work is at the correct height, and an arm with a clamp on the end. The frame is held in the clamp by means of an adjustable screw plate. You can turn the frame round to enable you to stitch comfortably on any part of the embroidery. A lever on the arm allows you to rotate the frame to have your work at the correct angle for stitching and to loosen the arm so that you can turn the frame over to finish off and start new threads, without taking the frame off the stand.

It is essential to have good light in which to stitch. If you are lucky enough to have time during the day, you can sit near a window, but if, like me, you can only grab an hour or two during the evenings, an anglepoise lamp fitted with a daylight bulb is a very good alternative to daylight. I am right-handed, so I have my light source coming over my left shoulder, so that as I stitch, my right hand does not cast a shadow on the area I am stitching. I have my lamp on a little table on my left-hand side, so that I can angle the light directly over my work. Of course, if you are left-handed, your light source will need to come from the right.

The author at work, using a home-made frame mounted in a Lowery stand, and an anglepoise lamp fitted with a daylight bulb.

Good light is essential for all types of needlework, but particularly for Mountmellick embroidery, because working white on white can be hard on your eyes. This is the embroidery from the cover of this book, showing dog roses and blackberries.

If you sit facing a table, the light can come from the front, facing you. At the moment I find that good light is better than magnification, but I might change my mind as I get older and my eyesight gets worse!

It is also very useful to have all the threads, scissors, needles and other items needed in a box or bag near to hand.

The most important thing is to be comfortable, so gather up all your materials, settle down and start stitching. Don't forget your glasses, if you wear them! I usually get all ready, get comfortable, reach for the needle and thread, and find that my glasses are still in my handbag!

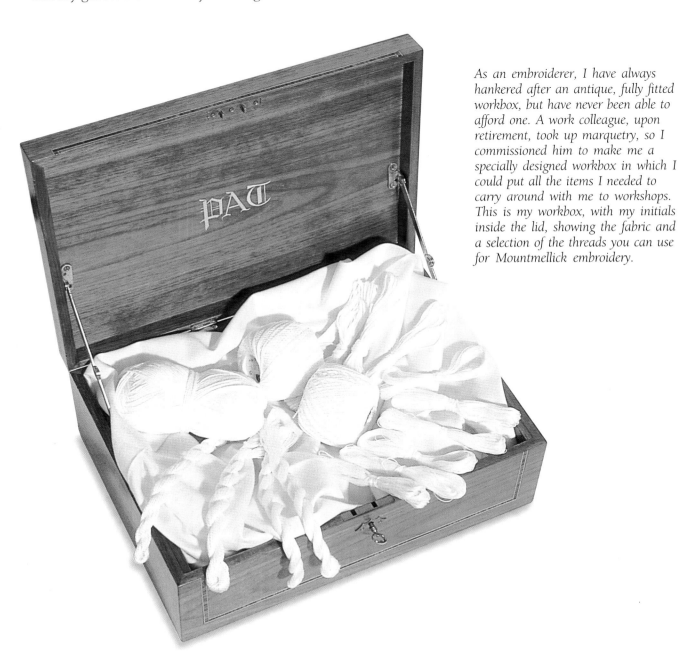

As an embroiderer, I have always hankered after an antique, fully fitted workbox, but have never been able to afford one. A work colleague, upon retirement, took up marquetry, so I commissioned him to make me a specially designed workbox in which I could put all the items I needed to carry around with me to workshops. This is my workbox, with my initials inside the lid, showing the fabric and a selection of the threads you can use for Mountmellick embroidery.

15

Stitches

This book contains thirteen stitches, which are shown step by step on pages 18–33. At the end of each stitch is a small motif showing how the stitch can be used. This sampler is the collection of all thirteen motifs. From left to right along the rows, the motifs show:

Wheat Ears: detached chain stitch. Stems: stem stitch.

Dog rose Petals: padded satin stitch. Rose centre: French knots. Main stem: Mountmellick stitch. Stem on the leaf: stem stitch. Leaves: buttonhole stitch.

Acorn Stem: palestrina knot stitch. Leaves: split stitch. Acorns: padded satin stitch. Acorn cups: French knots.

Holly Stem: cable plait stitch. Berries: satin stitch. Leaves: coral knot stitch.

Blackberries Main stem and leaf veins: chain stitch. Small stem: stem stitch. Leaves: couching. Berries: French knots and detached chain stitch.

Shamrock Stem: stem stitch. Shamrock leaves: satin stitch. Tendrils: couching.

Elderberries Stems: stem stitch. Main stem, berries and leaves: buttonhole stitch.

Ivy Stem: Portuguese knotted stem stitch. Leaves: split stitch. Berries: buttonhole stitch.

Vine leaves Stem: cable plait stitch. Leaves and tendrils: couching. Leaf veins: stem stitch.

Catkins Main stem: satin stitch. Small stem: stem stitch. Catkins: French knots. Small leaves: detached chain stitch.

Long-stemmed blackberries Main stem: Mountmellick stitch. Small stems and leaf veins: stem stitch. Leaves: couching. Blackberries: French knots and detached chain.

Daisy Petals: satin stitch. Daisy centre: French knots. Stem: cable plait stitch. Leaf: buttonhole stitch.

Grapes on vine Main stem: cable plait stitch. Small stem: stem stitch. Tendril: couching. Grapes: outlined in split stitch, padded, then padded satin stitch.

Couching

You will find that not many of the 'line' stitches, such as stem or chain stitch, go round tight curves or sharp angles. Couching is therefore a very useful stitch for wavy, curly or jagged lines. It is also useful for holding down a thick thread on a line, enabling you to use a very thick thread that might not like being pulled through the fabric too many times. If you are couching the thread, you only need to pull it through at the beginning and end of the line.

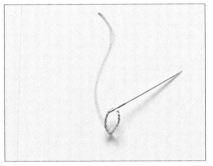

1. Bring the thick thread (shown in blue) up through the fabric at the start of the design.

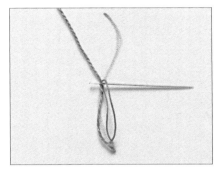

2. Bring the finer thread (shown in pink) up on one side of the thicker thread.

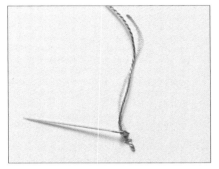

3. Take the needle down on the other side of the thicker thread and come up on the first side to start the second stitch.

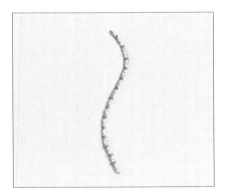

4. A finished line of couching stitches. Threads in different colours are used here for clarity, but in Mountmellick, both threads would be white.

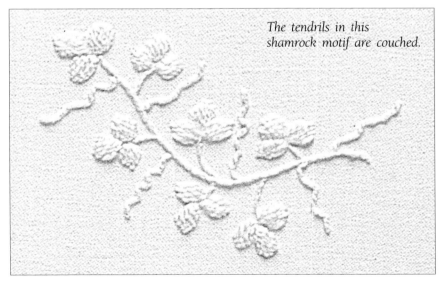

The tendrils in this shamrock motif are couched.

Split stitch

In this book, split stitch is used mainly to outline areas that are to be filled with satin or padded satin stitch. It makes a nice firm edge and will help to give a smooth, rounded effect to the petals. It can also be used on its own on wavy, curly or jagged lines in the same way as couching. The grapes on the vine shown below were all outlined in split stitch, then padded (see Padded satin stitch on page 28), then a final layer of satin stitch was added, completely covering the original split stitch outline. I have left some grapes unfinished so that the split stitch can be seen.

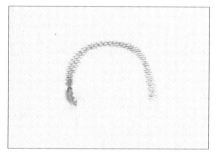

1. Bring the thread up at the beginning of the design and go down with a straight stitch.

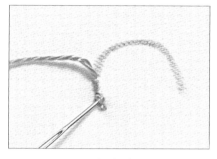

2. Come up a little further along the line. Take the needle back down near the end of the previous stitch to split it.

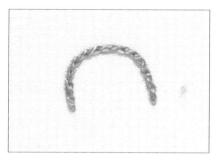

3. Repeat. A line of completed split stitches.

The grapes in this motif were outlined in split stitch, before being covered in padded satin stitch. Some of the outlines have been left uncovered.

Coral knot

This is another useful stitch for wavy, curly or jagged lines, especially if you make the knot on the points and angles of a jagged line, as on the holly leaves. You can space the knots very closely, or far apart, depending on the thickness of thread, the design and the effect you want to achieve. Right handers work from right to left, left handers from left to right. As I am right-handed, I have demonstrated this way, with apologies to left-handers!

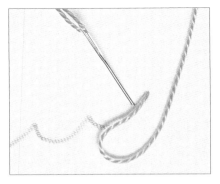

1. Come up on the right-hand side of the design. Lay the thread along the line of the design in the direction you are working, with the thread coming back towards you in an anticlockwise circle. Put the needle in above the thread, where you want your knot.

2. Pull the needle to the back, and before you have pulled all the thread through, bring the needle up again below the thread, and level with the point where you went down, making sure the needle comes up within the circle. Gently pull the thread up towards you, until it makes a knot.

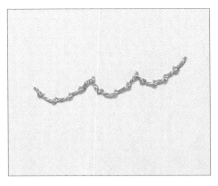

3. Continue in the same way all along the line, spacing the knots where you want them.

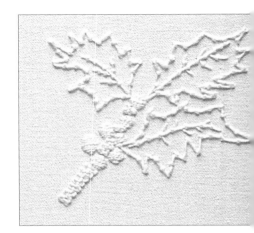

These holly leaves were worked in coral knot stitch, which is ideal for jagged lines.

Chain stitch

As the name implies, this stitch looks like a chain. It is made up of small links, which are known as detached chain stitch when separate, but in chain stitch are linked together to form a chain. Chain stitch is a line stitch – it is principally used on lines, though it can be used in other ways. You work downwards from the top of the line to the bottom, towards yourself.

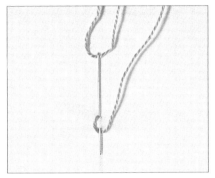

1. Come up from the back at the top of the design. Make an anticlockwise circle with the thread. Go back down the same hole. Come up a little way down the line, making sure the needle is inside the loop of thread.

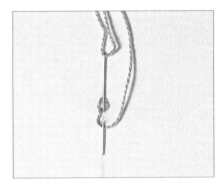

2. Pull the thread through to make a link. Go back down inside the first link in the same hole you came up in the previous step, and repeat.

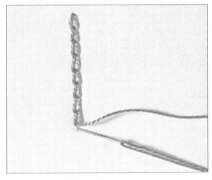

3. To end the chain, take the needle down outside the last link.

4. For detached chain stitch, after making one chain link, go down outside the link.

The ears of wheat in this design were worked in detached chain stitch.

French knots

French knots should look like a 'lady's bun hairstyle' – nice and round with a dimple in the middle. To achieve this effect, you should only wrap the thread round the needle once. To make knots of different sizes, you should use a thicker or a finer thread – rather than varying the number of wraps.

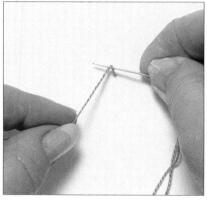 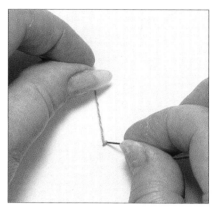 

1. Come up from the back where you want the knot to be. Hold the thread in your left hand. Put the needle on top of the thread and wrap the thread round it once.

2. Re-enter the fabric very close to where you came out. When the needle is halfway down, gently pull the thread taut.

3. Push the needle down and pull through to make a knot. The finished knot should look like a little circle with a dimple in the middle.

4. A cluster of knots worked.

Stem stitch

This is another line stitch, especially good for stems or branches. The finished effect should look like a rope. It is very effective on straight lines, but can also be used on curved lines. It works best on lines that curve from right to left. It does not work well on very tight curves or circles. Work from the bottom of a line up towards the top, away from yourself. The length of the stitches you make will depend on the thickness of the thread. When using a fine thread, make the stitches small, and when using a thicker thread, make them longer.

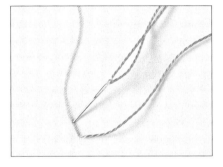

1. Come up at the bottom of the design. Keep the thread to the right of the line you're working on. Go down again a little way along the line.

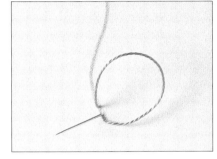

2. Come up again half way between where you came up and where you went down, and pull through. Steps 1 and 2 apply only for the first stitch of the design.

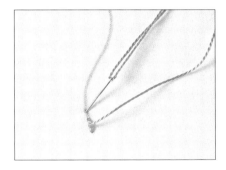

3. Keep the thread to the right of the line you're working on. Go down a little way above the top of the previous stitch.

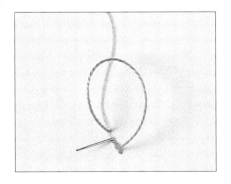

4. Come up through the same hole as the top of the previous stitch.

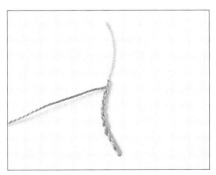

5. Continue, repeating steps 3 and 4.

The smaller stem of these catkins is worked in stem stitch.

Portuguese knotted stem stitch

This stitch can be used where you want a thick line; it is thicker than stem stitch. It can also be very useful where you need a more textured stem or branch. It is worked from the bottom of a line to the top, away from yourself. It looks a little complicated, but you soon get in a rhythm and this can be a very therapeutic, soothing stitch to do!

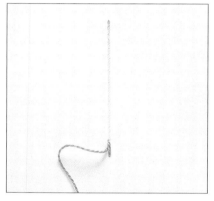

1. Come up at the bottom of the design. Go down a little way above it, keeping the thread to the right, and come up halfway between where you came up and went down (as for stem stitch).

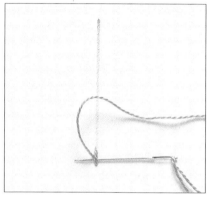

2. You now need to wrap this stitch twice. Keep the thread to the left. Form a clockwise loop and pass the needle from right to left under your first stitch, below the loop. That is wrap one.

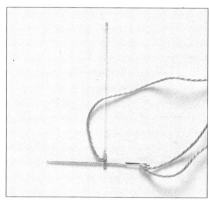

3. Pull the thread upwards to tighten the knot. Go round again and take the needle under the stitch, below the first wrap.

4. Make sure your second wrap is below the first. Pull the thread upwards to tighten the knot. (Steps 1 to 4 are for the first stitch only).

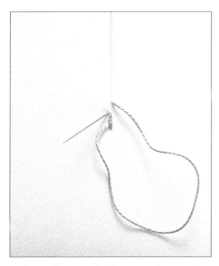

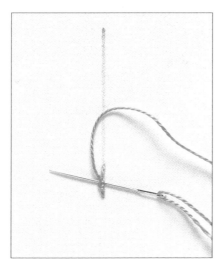

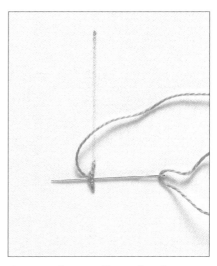

5. Go down a little way above the top of the previous stitch. Come up just to the left-hand side and level with the top of the previous stitch. The bottom of the new stitch should overlap the top of the previous stitch.

6. Pass your needle under the two overlapping stitches from right to left and pull taut. This makes wrap one.

7. Pass the needle under the two overlapping stitches from right to left, and below the first wrap. Pull taut again.

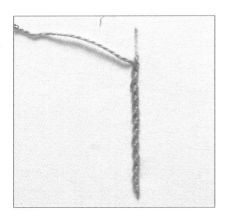

8. Repeat steps 5 to 7 to the end of the line. Then take the thread through to the back and finish off.

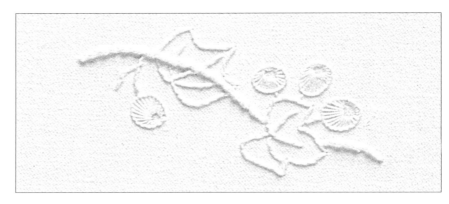

Portuguese knotted stem stitch is ideal for the thick stem in this ivy design.

Buttonhole stitch

This stitch is used to edge your finished projects before adding the knitted fringe, but I have also used it as a stitch in its own right, mainly on leaves. It is worked from left to right. The leaves were worked up one side and down the other, sharing the middle line, thus creating a vein in the middle. The berries were worked in a circular way, the top of all the stitches sharing the same middle hole.

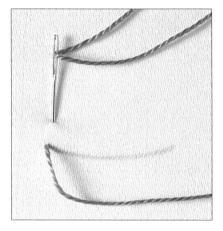 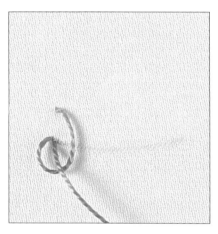 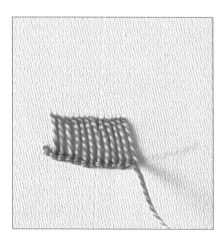

1. Come up on your design line. Go down the desired stitch length up from the line. The thread goes round in an anticlockwise circle.

2. Come up on the bottom line to the right of where you started, inside the anticlockwise loop. Pull through and pull taut so that the stitch lies flat on the fabric.

3. Repeat steps 1 and 2 to the end of the line. Finish off by going down to the right of your last stitch, on the design line.

The elderberries and leaves in this motif were worked in buttonhole stitch.

Satin stitch

The beauty of satin stitch lies in its simplicity: long, straight stitches lying next to one another with a smooth, even edge. However, the simpler a stitch, the easier it is to see mistakes, so great care must be taken with satin stitch. Take your time and do not rush! One of the ways to achieve a smooth edge is to outline the desired area in split stitch first. This gives you a line to work on. Another tip is to get the angle of the stitch right. Do not come up at the top or bottom of the petal, but about half or a third of the way up. Get your angle right, then work up to the top, then down to the bottom. In this book, satin stitch has been used mainly for flower petals.

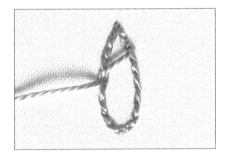

1. Outline in split stitch first. Start in the middle of the design. This helps you to set an angle for the stitches which you then follow throughout. Come up on the outside of the outline on one side of the design. Hold the thread until you are happy with the angle the stitch will make.

2. Go down on the opposite side of the design. Come up again on the first side, outside the outline as before.

3. Repeat along the design, making sure the stitches lie as close as possible to one another, and keep to the same angle.

Satin stitch was used to create the smooth petals in this daisy motif.

4. Go back to the middle where you started, and fill in the rest of the design.

Padded satin stitch

Padded satin stitch gives a much higher relief than flat satin stitch. It is worked in the same way, but is padded first to give it height. This padding is worked inside the split stitch edge using the same threads as you use for stitching. Do not be tempted to use wadding or cotton wool – it will not work. When you have embroidered some of the stems and leaves in your design, you will have thread left in the needle that has been through the fabric a few times and got 'tired' and 'fluffy'. Use this to edge and pad some of the areas where you will be using padded satin stitch. This padding takes a long time and can be tedious if done all at once. Using the ends of the threads and doing it a bit at a time takes the tedium out of it. It feels really good to have most of the padding done so that you can use your newest threads to work the final layer.

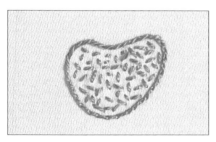

1. After outlining the shape with split stitch, fill in the area with tiny straight stitches placed at random (seeding stitches).

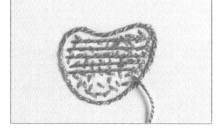

2. Cover the seeding stitches with long straight stitches, still within the outline.

3. The last layer of straight padding stitches must be at right angles to the direction you want your final satin stitches to take.

4. Fill in with satin stitches, starting and finishing outside the outline, to cover it.

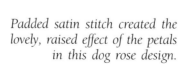

Padded satin stitch created the lovely, raised effect of the petals in this dog rose design.

Palestrina knot stitch

This is a lovely textured line stitch that can be used for stems and branches that need a knobbly look. It is also known as double knot stitch. My personal preference is for the knots to be quite close together, but of course you can place them further apart if you like. This stitch looks particularly good in a thick thread. It is worked from top to bottom, down the line towards yourself.

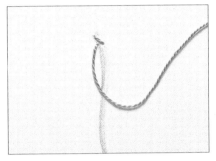

1. Work from top to bottom. Come out at the top of the line. Go down just below this point and to the right, to make a little diagonal stitch. Come up on the line again, below the first point. Keep the thread coming down towards you.

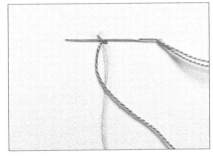

2. Pass the needle right to left under the diagonal stitch, to make a wrap.

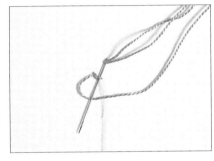

3. Make an anticlockwise circle with your thread and pass the needle top to bottom under the original diagonal stitch, below the wrap, making sure the thread is under the needle. Pull taut to make a knot.

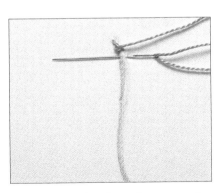

4. Keeping the thread up out of the way, go down to the right of the line, and come up on the line, to make another diagonal stitch.

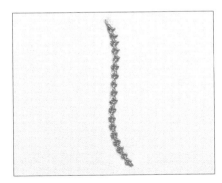

5. Pull through and repeat steps 2, 3 and 4 to make a line of knots. Space them out as desired.

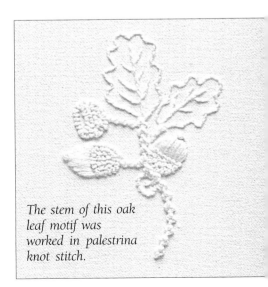

The stem of this oak leaf motif was worked in palestrina knot stitch.

Mountmellick stitch

Mountmellick is another line stitch but is wider than stem or
chain, so it can be used on thick stems. It is a bold, raised stitch.
One side of the stitch has a straight edge, the other has a little
'leg' that looks a little like a thorn, so this stitch can be used very
well for the stems of roses or blackberries. It is worked from top to
bottom down the line towards you.

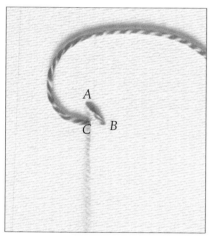

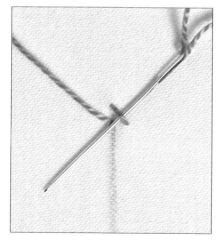

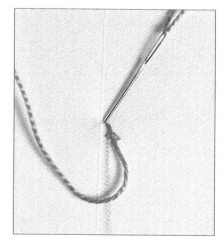

1. Come out at the top of the line
(A). Make a diagonal stitch to the
right and go down at (B). Come
up back on the line below the
starting point (C). Keep the
thread out of the way at the top.

2. Pass the needle from top to
bottom under the diagonal stitch,
keeping the thread out of the way
to the left of the needle.

3. Now take the thread round in
a clockwise direction. Go down
the same hole you first came out
of (A).

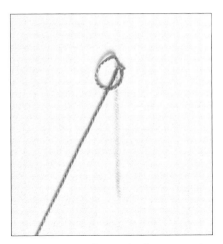

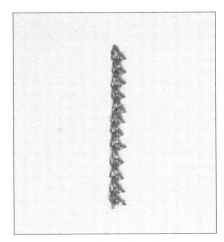

4. Come up through the second hole on the line (C). Make sure you are inside the loop of thread, and gently pull taut. This will form a triangle, with the straight edge on the left and the little 'leg' on the right.

5. Start the next stitch with a diagonal stitch (as in step 1) and repeat steps 2 and 3, as before, making sure that when you go down at A, it is inside the triangular stitch you have just made. (C of your first stitch becomes the A of your second stitch). Come up at C of the second stitch, again making sure you are inside the clockwise circle of thread. You are now at step 4 of your second stitch. This C will now become A of your third stitch.

6. Continue down the line, and finish by going to the back just below the straight edge of the triangle.

Mountmellick stitch is ideal for thick, thorny stems like the one in this blackberry design.

Cable plait stitch

This is a wide stitch useful for thick stems. It is made between two parallel lines that form a channel. I have used it for the main, thick trunk of a vine. It can also be used around the edge of a project instead of buttonhole stitch. Let the stitch sit on the surface of the fabric, do not pull it too tightly or it will just fold up into the middle of the channel. This is a very pretty stitch – one of my favourites. It is also another rhythmical, therapeutic stitch. It is worked from top to bottom down the channel towards yourself.

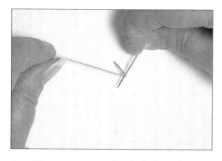

1. Come up on the left-hand line. Hold the thread in your left hand. Put the needle under the thread pointing towards 'eleven o'clock' and turn it anticlockwise towards you.

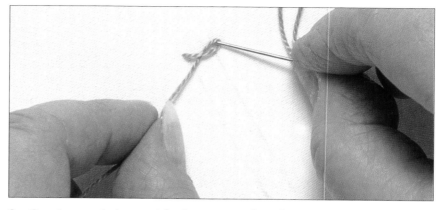

2. Continue twisting anticlockwise to make a loop where the exiting thread is on top of the long thread. Push the needle down on the right-hand line, inside the loop you have made.

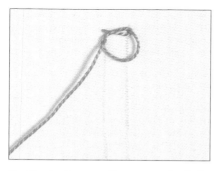

3. Push the needle up on the left-hand line. Make sure your thread is under your needle. Pull the thread taut round the needle. Pull the needle through to the front.

Cable plait stitch is ideal for thick stems like the one in this vine leaf design.

4. Pull the thread through, but do not pull too tight. The stitch should lie on the surface of the fabric.

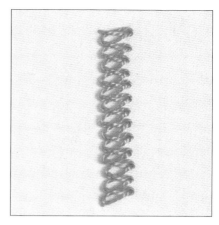

5. Repeat down between the two lines.

I live in Kent, where the hop fields are disappearing rapidly, so I thought it would be nice to include a design based on hops.

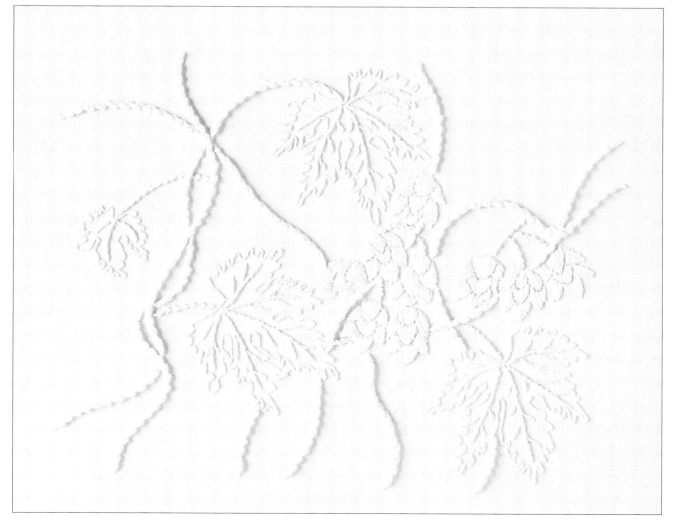

Knitted fringes

One of the main characteristics of Mountmellick work is the knitted fringe. It would be impossible to knit the length of fringe needed, especially on large items such as a tablecloth or bedspread, so the fringe is knitted sideways. It is knitted in multiples of three stitches, casting on enough stitches for the required width of fringe. There is nothing worse than a mean, sparse fringe – it needs to be full and weighty to look good – so it is knitted in multiples of thread simultaneously, usually three or four, from separate balls of yarn. The finer the thread you use, the more threads you need in the multiple. For the fringe shown below, I cast on twelve stitches. You can use any number that is divisible by three.

Casting on

You can cast on in your usual way, but if you cast on with the one needle method shown below, you can cast on using two needles held together as one. This will make the cast-on stitches a little looser, so that it is easier to knit the first row.

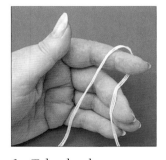

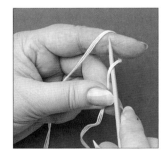

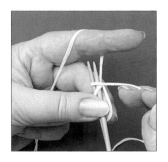

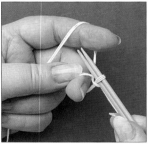

1. Take the three threads in your left hand as shown. The thread goes over the index finger and between the thumb and third finger.

2. Hold the thread. Insert two needles under the thread as shown.

3. Hold the needles in your left hand and loop thread from the balls right to left, anticlockwise, round the needles.

4. Pull the needles through the loop.

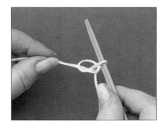

5. Pull the loop tight around the needles. Cast on twelve stitches in this way, and then pull out one of the needles ready to start knitting.

Knitting

6. Put the right-hand needle into the first loop on the left-hand needle.

7. Wind the thread right to left, anticlockwise, round the needle.

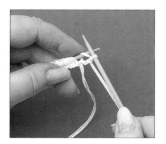

8. Pull the thread through the loop.

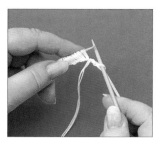

9. Slip the loop off the left-hand needle.

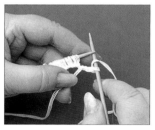

10. Make one by bringing the thread under the right-hand needle so that it is between the two needles.

11. Knit two together: put the right-hand needle through two loops on the left-hand needle and repeat steps 7 to 9.

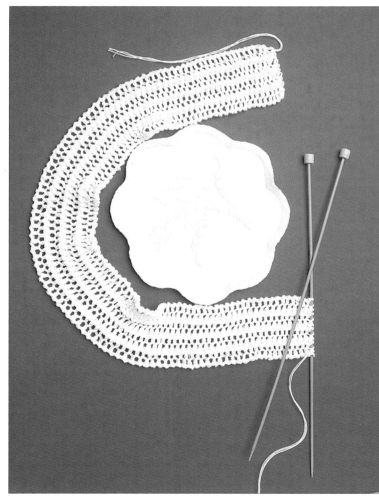

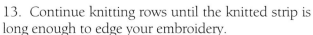

12. Repeat steps 6 to 11 to the end of the row.

13. Continue knitting rows until the knitted strip is long enough to edge your embroidery.

Casting off

14. Knit one on to the right-hand needle.

15. Knit a second stitch in the same way.

16. Put the left-hand needle through the first stitch.

17. Take the first stitch over the second and...

18. ...slip the stitch off the needle.

19. Continue until only five stitches are left on the left-hand needle. Cut off the thread.

20. Take the right-hand needle out, take the thread through the last stitch and pull tight.

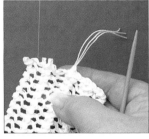

21. Take the left-hand needle out of the last five stitches.

22. Unravel the edge with a needle. Pull out the first stitch.

23. The fringe develops as more and more stitches are unravelled.

24. Stitch the fringe on to the finished piece.

A small mat with a vine leaf design. The buttonhole edge is completed, ready for the fringe to be sewn on to it.

The vine leaf mat with the knitted fringe sewn in place.

Getting started
Transferring a design

To avoid spoiling your book, and because you will find it easier to trace, I suggest that you photocopy the design you like (see Patterns on pages 55–63). At this stage you can also choose whether or not to enlarge or reduce the size. Once you have the photocopy, you can either trace this on to greaseproof paper using a black felt tip pen, or you can use the photocopy itself. You will find that the light shines through the greaseproof paper more than through the photocopy paper.

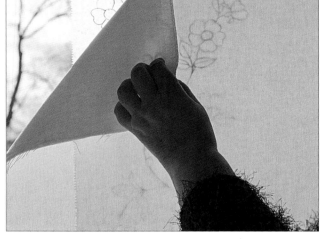

1. Place the design on a lightbox, or tape it to a window, as shown. Tape the fabric over the top.

2. Trace off the design using a water soluble pen.

Dressing the frame

There are many different types of frame on the market. I am going to show you how to dress two: a slate frame and a home-made 'picture frame' type. The most important thing to remember is to tension the fabric equally in both directions, ensuring that it is drum tight before you start stitching.

A slate frame

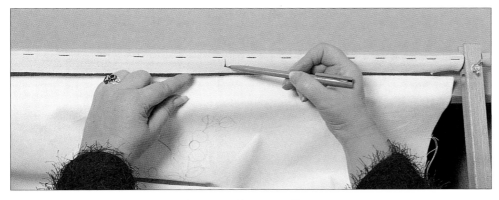

1. Mark the centre of the webbing on the top roller with a permanent marker. Find the centre of the width of the fabric.

2. Pin the fabric to the webbing, to keep it in place. From the centre towards one side, using backstitch, sew the fabric to the webbing. Fold over the sides of the fabric to tidy up the edges and to make it strong enough to attach to the frame.

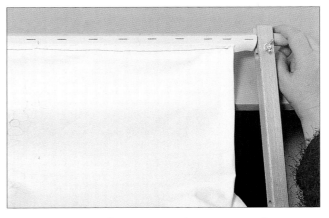

3. Start again at the centre and sew outwards towards the other side. Repeat steps 1 to 3 at the bottom roller. Loosen the wing nuts of the bottom roller.

4. Roll the bottom roller round to take up the excess fabric.

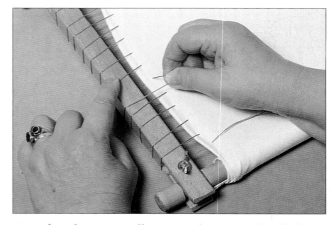

5. Take a long piece of doubled crochet cotton and tie the ends. Come up through the side of the fabric, where it is folded over. Lace the fabric round the sides of the frame so that it is tight horizontally. Keep hold of the thread with your left hand to keep it under tension.

6. Before fastening off, start at the top and pull the lacing one stitch at a time until it is evenly tight all the way down. Pull each thread another time to tighten further. Then lace up the other side of the fabric in the same way.

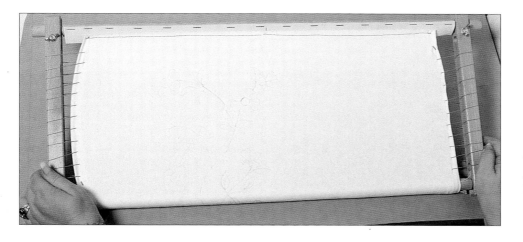

7. The framed fabric. When the frame is properly dressed, the fabric should be drum tight ready for stitching.

A home-made frame

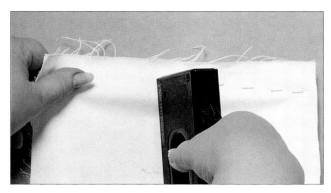

1. Starting in the middle on the top of the frame, staple the fabric to the frame from the centre outwards. Afterwards, start from the centre again and staple out to the other side.

2. Pull the fabric tight and staple it to the bottom of the frame. Start in the middle and work out to each side in turn.

3. Next staple the sides of the frame in the same way. Staple one side and then pull the fabric tight and staple the side opposite it, until all the fabric is drum tight.

Threading a needle

Because the eyes of needles are always flat, flatten the end of your thread by clenching it between your teeth. The flattened end should go through the eye.

Beginning and ending your threads

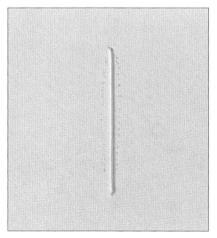

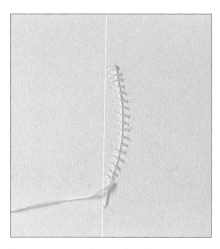

1. Knot the end of your thread. Put your needle down through the fabric from front to back, about 10cm (4in) away from where you want to start your design. The knot at the front is known as the waste knot. Bring the needle up at the start of your design (this vine stem will be worked from top to bottom).

2. The thread at the back should be in an area you are going to work, so that it will be caught up by your stitching.

3. Begin stitching the design. This picture shows the thread at the back of the fabric after the stem of the vine has been stitched. The thread is now caught up in the finished stitching.

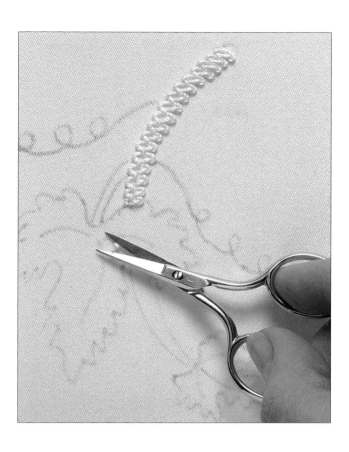

4. When you have finished stitching, snip off the waste knot. The stitches will still be secure, because the thread at the back is caught up in the stitching.

5. To finish off, take the thread through some of the stitches at the back, and knot.

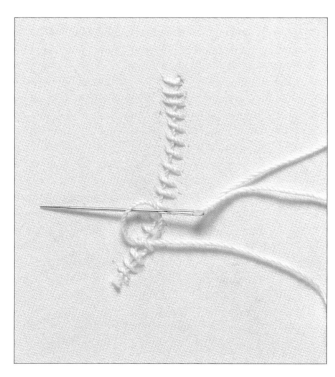

Dog Roses and Blackberries

This project and the following one will include all the stitches demonstrated in this book.

As a general rule, when embroidering a piece of work, begin with items that are in the background and work towards items that are in the foreground of the design. It is a lot easier to embroider over stems than to try to slot in a stem behind foreground leaves or flowers that have already been worked.

This project includes Mountmellick stitch for the thicker stems and palestrina and stem stitch for the finer stems. Split stitch and padded satin stitch are used for the rose, coral knot for some leaves and stem stitch for others, and French knots for the centres of the roses and the blackberries. Detached chain stitch is used for the tops of the blackberries.

Embroider the stems first, stitching the ones furthest away from you first, and working up to the ones in front. Don't forget to use the 'fluffy' end threads to pad the areas that will be in padded satin stitch, such as the petals of the rose, the buds and the rosehips.

Opposite
The pattern for the Dog Roses and Blackberries embroidery

44

1. Work the background stems first, and then any stems crossing over them. The thickest stems are Mountmellick stitch, the medium ones are palestrina, and the finest ones are stem stitch. Outline the petals in split stitch. With the fluffy, over-used ends of the thread, begin the first stage of padding inside the petals by placing seeding stitches at random. This dog rose is shown with the seeding stitches in progress.

2. When this first layer of seeding stitches is complete, you can begin placing padding stitches on top. These are long, straight stitches placed inside the split stitch outline, shown here in the dog rose from the right-hand side of the design.

3. Continue the padding stitches, as in this half-open dog rose. Each layer of padding stitches should be placed at right angles to the layer before. The last layer of padding stitches should be at right angles to the direction in which you want the final satin stitches to go.

Opposite
The first stage of embroidering in progress, with the stems worked and the outlining complete. Some of the seeding stitches and padding stitches have been started.

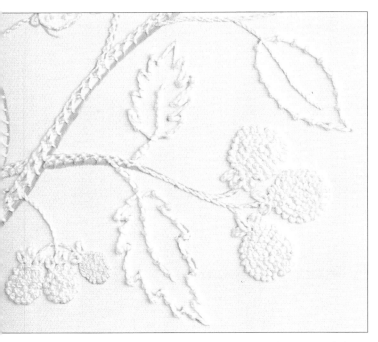

4. Now work the larger leaves in coral knot and the smaller ones in stem stitch, and the blackberries in French knots, as shown here. Work the 'tops' of the blackberries in detached chain stitch.

5. Continue adding layers of padding. The left-hand petal of this dog rose has its final layer of padding stitches. The satin stitches will be at right angles to these. The middle petal has the beginnings of the final layer of padding stitches.

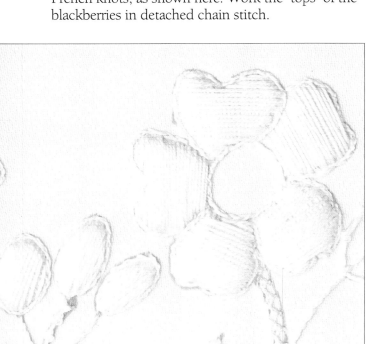

6. This dog rose and rosehips are shown with all their layers of padding completed, ready for the satin stitch.

Opposite
Dog Roses and Blackberries

The finished embroidery. The satin stitch layer has been added to the rose petals, buds and rosehips. Satin stitch has been used to work the sepals at the bases of the flowers shown from the side. A single French knot has been added to the top of each rosehip. The centres of the flowers have been filled with French knots.

Poppies, Corn and Daisies

This project will include couching and detached chain stitch on the corn, stem stitch and Portuguese knotted stem stitch on some of the stems, palestrina and cable plait on some of the thicker stems, buttonhole on poppies and couching on the leaves. The daisy petals are worked in satin stitch with the centres worked in French knots. The daisy petals look slightly raised because a thick thread is used, and because the satin stitch goes over the outline; no padding is used here. The poppy bud next to the poppy at the top of the design is worked in padded satin stitch to give it body.

Opposite
The pattern for the Poppies, Corn and Daisies embroidery

1. Work the background stems first, then those nearer to the foreground. Here the thicker stem in palestrina knot stitch is worked over the top of the finer stem in stem stitch.

2. Outline the daisy petals using split stitch.

3. Outline the bud in split stitch and use any fluffy, over-used thread to begin the seeding stitches inside the outline as shown.

5. Couch the leaves as shown. Couching is the ideal stitch for creating the wavy lines of the leaves in this design.

4. Continue outlining the daisies in split stitch. You can use fluffy, over-used threads for outlining, as the outline will later be covered by satin stitch.

6. Work the ears of corn using detached chain stitch, and use couching for the wisps protruding from the ears.

The Poppies, Corn and Daisies embroidery with the background and middle distance in progress. The stems, worked in four different stitches and crossing over one another, create a wonderful textured effect.

Poppies, Corn and Daisies

The finished embroidery. The daisies have been worked with satin stitch. The outline under the satin stitch gives the petals a slightly raised effect, but it is not as pronounced as in padded satin stitch. The centres of the poppies and some of the daisies have been filled with French knots. The poppy petals have been created using buttonhole stitches.

54

Patterns

These patterns can be reduced or enlarged on a photocopier before transferring on to the fabric (see page 38).

The pattern for the harp design on page 1

The pattern for the passionflower design on pages 2–3

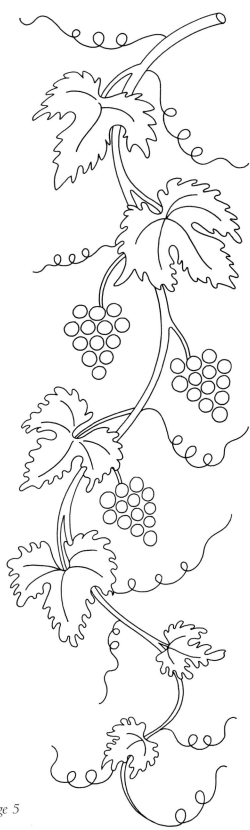

The pattern for the vine design on page 5

58

The pattern for the convolvulus design on page 7

The pattern for the sampler on pages 16–17

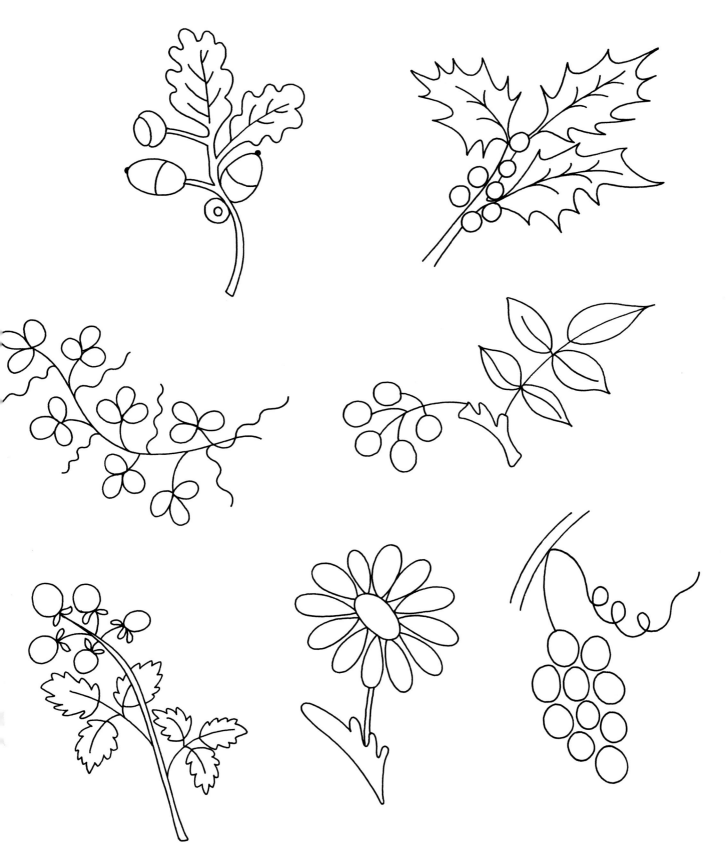

The pattern for the cover design, which also appears on page 14

Index